D1507658

Superstars of the DENVER BRONCOS

by Matt Scheff

AMICUS HIGH INTEREST ✦ AMICUS INK

Amicus High Interest and
Amicus Ink are imprints of Amicus
P.O. Box 1329, Mankato, MN 56002
www.amicuspublishing.us

Library of Congress Cataloging-in-Publication Data
Scheff, Matt.
  Superstars of the Denver Broncos / Matt Scheff.
     pages cm. -- (Pro sports superstars)
  Includes index.
  ISBN 978-1-60753-524-9 (hardcover) -- ISBN 978-1-60753-554-6 (eBook)
  ISBN 978-1-68152-061-2 (paperback)
  1. Denver Broncos (Football team)--History--Juvenile literature. 2.
Football players--United States--Biography--Juvenile literature. I. Title.
  GV956.D37.S34 2013
  796.332'640978883--dc23
                          2013006831

Photo Credits: Tom DiPace/AP Images, cover; Jack Dempsey/AP Images,
2, 18, 21; Eric Bakke/AP Images, 5; FK/AP Images, 7; Four Seam Images/AP
Images, 8, 22; Al Golub/AP Images, 11; G. Newman Lowrance/AP Images,
12; Chuck Burton/AP Images, 15; Kevin Terrell/AP Images, 17

Produced for Amicus by The Peterson Publishing Company
and Red Line Editorial.

Editor: Jenna Gleisner
Designer: Becky Daum

Printed in Malaysia

HC 10 9 8 7 6 5 4
PB 10 9 8 7 6 5 4 3 2 1

TABLE OF CONTENTS

MEET THE DENVER BRONCOS

The Denver Broncos have played since 1960. They started in a league called the **AFL**. They joined the **NFL** in 1970. The Broncos have won two Super Bowls. They have had many stars. Here are some of the best.

FLOYD LITTLE

Floyd Little was a great runner. He was fast. Little was hard to tackle. He led pro football in **rushing** in 1971. Little went to three **Pro Bowls**.

JOHN ELWAY

John Elway was a great **quarterback**. He had a strong arm. He was also a good runner. Elway led the Broncos to five Super Bowls. They won two of them.

Elway was the NFL MVP in 1987.

STEVE ATWATER

Steve Atwater was a great tackler. He hit hard. Atwater was best at stopping the run. He also knocked down passes. Atwater played in seven straight Pro Bowls from 1990 to 1996.

SHANNON SHARPE

Shannon Sharpe was a great **tight end**. He blocked well. He was great at catching passes. He helped the Broncos win two Super Bowls in a row in 1997 and 1998.

Sharpe went to eight Pro Bowls.

GARY ZIMMERMAN

Gary Zimmerman was a strong blocker. He protected passers. He helped runners cut through the other team. Zimmerman was named to the NFL All-Decade team in the 1980s and 1990s.

TERRELL DAVIS

Terrell Davis only played four full seasons. But they were great. He was fast and powerful. He knew how to score. Davis helped the Broncos win two Super Bowls.

Davis was the NFL MVP in 1998.

Smith led the NFL with 113 catches in 2001.

ROD SMITH

Rod Smith played 12 seasons with Denver. He was great at catching passes. He was fast. Smith has the most catches in team history. He won two Super Bowls with the Broncos.

VON MILLER

Von Miller is a star on **defense**. He joined the Broncos in 2011. He is quick and strong. He loves to sack the quarterback.

The Broncos have had some great stars. Some have made the Hall of Fame. Who will be the next star?

TEAM FAST FACTS

Founded: 1960

Nicknames: Orange Crush

Home Stadium: Sports Authority Field at Mile High (Denver, Colorado)

Super Bowl Titles: 2 (1997 and 1998)

Hall of Fame Players: 6, including Floyd Little, John Elway, Shannon Sharpe, and Gary Zimmerman

WORDS TO KNOW

AFL – the American Football League; a league that played in the 1960s

defense – the group of players that tries to stop the other team from scoring

MVP – Most Valuable Player; an honor given to the best player each season

NFL – National Football League; the league pro football players play in

Pro Bowl – the NFL's all-star game

quarterback – a player whose main jobs are to lead the offense and throw passes

rushing – running with the ball

tight end – a player whose main jobs are to catch passes and block

LEARN MORE

Books

Frisch, Aaron. *Denver Broncos*. Mankato, MN: Creative Education, 2011.

Omoth, Tyler. *The Story of the Denver Broncos*. Mankato, MN: Creative Education, 2010.

Web Sites

Denver Broncos—Official Site
http://www.denverbroncos.com/
Watch video clips and view photos of the Denver Broncos.

NFL.com
http://nfl.com
Check out pictures and your favorite football players' stats.

NFL Rush
http://www.nflrush.com
Play games and learn how to be a part of NFL PLAY 60.

INDEX